Pebble®

BUSINESS LEADERS

Sam
Walton

by Erika L. Shores

Consulting Editor: Gail Saunders-Smith, PhD

Consultant: Alan Dranow
Senior Director, Walmart Heritage Group
Bentonville, Arkansas

CAPSTONE PRESS
a capstone imprint

Pebble Books are published by Capstone Press,
1710 Roe Crest Drive, North Mankato, Minnesota 56003
www.capstonepub.com

Library of Congress Cataloging-in-Publication Data
Cataloging-in-publication information is on file with the Library of Congress.
ISBN 978-1-4765-9642-6 (library binding)
ISBN 978-1-4765-9646-4 (paperback)
ISBN 978-1-4765-9650-1 (eBook PDF)

Note to Parents and Teachers

The Business Leaders set supports national social studies standards
related to people, places, and environments. This book describes
and illustrates Sam Walton. The images support early readers in
understanding the text. The repetition of words and phrases helps
early readers learn new words. This book also introduces early
readers to subject-specific vocabulary words, which are defined
in the Glossary section. Early readers may need assistance to read
some words and to use the Table of Contents, Glossary, Read More,
Internet Sites, and Index sections of the book.

Printed in the United States of America in North Mankato, Minnesota.
092013   007764CGS14

Table of Contents

Sam was born in Kingfisher, Oklahoma, in 1918.

1918

born in
Oklahoma

Early Years

Sam Walton was the founder of Walmart stores. He was born March 29, 1918, in Oklahoma. His parents were Thomas and Nancy Walton.

Sam's high school photo in 1936

1918
born in Oklahoma

1940
graduates from the University of Missouri

6

Sam and his family moved to Missouri when he was 5. Sam went to high school in Columbia, Missouri. He starred on the football team. In 1940 Sam graduated from the University of Missouri.

Sam and his family in the 1950s

1918
born in
Oklahoma

1940
graduates from the
University of Missouri

1943
marries
Helen Robson

Young Adult

After college Sam went to work for J. C. Penney department stores in Iowa. Then in 1943 Sam married Helen Robson. They had four children.

A Walton's five-and-dime store in 1951

1918
born in
Oklahoma

1940
graduates from the
University of Missouri

1943
marries
Helen Robson

1945
buys Ben
Franklin store

10

Sam bought a Ben Franklin "five-and-dime" store in 1945. Sam's stores offered goods at a lower cost than anywhere else. Sam ran 15 Ben Franklins by the 1960s.

1918	**1940**	**1943**	**1945**
born in Oklahoma	graduates from the University of Missouri	marries Helen Robson	buys Ben Franklin store

Life's Work

Sam decided he wanted to open discount stores in small towns. In 1962 Sam started his own company. The first Walmart store was in Rogers, Arkansas.

1962

opens first Walmart
in Arkansas

A Walmart store in 1977

1918
born in
Oklahoma

1940
graduates from the
University of Missouri

1943
marries
Helen Robson

1945
buys Ben
Franklin store

14

Other companies would not open big stores in small towns. They believed too few people would shop there. Sam proved them wrong. By 1977, 190 Walmart stores were in small towns.

1962

opens first Walmart
in Arkansas

1918
born in
Oklahoma

1940
graduates from the
University of Missouri

1943
marries
Helen Robson

1945
buys Ben
Franklin store

Sam sold goods at low prices. He kept prices low by buying a lot of goods. He stored goods at warehouses. Walmart could charge customers less to buy goods.

1962

opens first Walmart
in Arkansas

Sam meets with his employees in 1990

1918	**1940**	**1943**	**1945**
born in Oklahoma	graduates from the University of Missouri	marries Helen Robson	buys Ben Franklin store

Sam valued his employees. Their work made Walmart successful. Sam tried to visit each store at least once a year.

1962

opens first Walmart
in Arkansas

1918	**1940**	**1943**	**1945**
born in Oklahoma	graduates from the University of Missouri	marries Helen Robson	buys Ben Franklin store

Later Life

By 1992 there were 1,735 Walmart stores. That year Sam received the Medal of Freedom. He died April 5, 1992. People remember Sam for bringing low-cost goods to millions of people.

1962
opens first Walmart in Arkansas

1992
receives Medal of Freedom

1992
dies on April 5

Glossary

college—a school students go to after high school

discount—a lowering in the usual cost of something

employee—a person who works for a company, store, or business

founder—a person who sets up or starts a company, business, or organization

Medal of Freedom—a medal the president gives to someone for his or her great works

Critical Thinking Using the Common Core

1. Sam founded Walmart stores. What does it mean to found something? What clues from the text help you figure out the word's meaning? (Key Ideas and Details)

2. Sam wanted to keep the prices of his goods low for his customers. Describe two ways Sam did this. Look back on the photos and text to find your answer. (Key Ideas and Details)

Read More

Kesselring, Mari. *Arkansas.* Mankato, Minn.: Child's World, 2010.

Mara, Wil. *Sam Walton: Rethinking Retail.* A True Book. New York: Children's Press, 2014.

Reynolds, Mattie. *Super-Smart Shopping: An Introduction to Financial Literacy.* Start Smart, Money. South Egremont, Mass.: Red Chair Press, 2013.

Internet Sites

FactHound offers a safe, fun way to find Internet sites related to this book. All of the sites on FactHound have been researched by our staff.

Here's all you do:

Visit *www.facthound.com*

Type in this code: 9781476596426

Check out projects, games and lots more at
www.capstonekids.com

Index

Word Count: 247
Grade: 1
Early-Intervention Level: 20

Editorial Credits

Michelle Hasselius, editor; Lori Bye, designer; Tracy Cummins, media researcher; Jennifer Walker, production specialist

Photo Credits

Charley Blackmore: www.kewpie.net, 6; Corbis: © Louie Psihoyos, cover; Dreamstime: Lynn Watson, 1; Getty Images: Diana Walker/Time Life Pictures, 20; Shutterstock: Veerachai Viteeman, cover; Walmart Corporation, 12, 16; The Walmart Museum, Bentonville, AR: © Wal-Mart Stores, Inc, 4, 8, 10, 14, 18